501 Terribly Good Dad Jokes!

Over 500 of The Worst - But Best - Dad Jokes, Puns and Knee Slappers for Kids and the Entire Family (Father's Day Special)

Old Chap Entertainment

Table of Contents

Introduction

Father's Day is a great occasion celebrated all around the globe to honor that special man in everyone's life - our dads! Dads hold a special place in our hearts, and Father's Day has been the time to celebrate them since the Middle Ages. After all, dads serve as examples of strength and responsibility, show us how to be independent and confident, and are some of our main supporters through life!

So, what do dads do best? We got a lot of answers when we reached out to kids. Some said their Dad spent a lot of time at the office, while other dads watched football. Some dads play soccer, and some dads fix cars. But there's one universal thing that's as loved as it is feared — the dawn of Dad jokes!

This book lists some of the most excellent dad jokes from a wide variety of sources to share with your Dad (or other father figures!) on Father's Day — and every day of the year!

Next time Dad cracks a joke, you'll be ready with one of your own. So flip open the pages, check out our guides, and let's get punny!

Who is this book for?

This book might be dedicated to dads, but it is good, clean fun for the entire family! Kids and teens usually cringe when their dads make terrible (that are so bad they're good!) jokes, and this book can allow them to get their own back! Moms might even want to take a turn too!

There are many benefits to sharing jokes in general and even more so in sharing humor as a family!

- Jokes can be positive for your <u>family's health</u>!: There have been several studies that link a sense of humor with coping skills. Laughter releases endorphins in the brain, which are known as the feel-good brain chemicals. These hormones mean humor can improve self-esteem or even help against mood disorders! Like many other skills, children learn about fun through social interaction. Sharing jokes with family can be the first step of a well-rounded sense of humor, strengthening your familial bonds and help ease a child's anxiety or grumpiness!

- Jokes help refine <u>verbal skills</u>!: Puns and jokes can be bite-sized lessons in spelling, homophones, and etymology. Even cheesy jokes can be a learning opportunity!

- Jokes can elevate <u>social standing</u>: A well-placed joke can be the foundation of a new! Children who share and enjoy jokes can start conversations with their peers more easily. Having a head start by practicing with family can arm a child with social tools, especially if they have problems in that area!

- Jokes can improve your <u>memory</u>: A good joke can make a concept easier to remember. Math, science, and history jokes can help your child remember something they otherwise would have trouble to grasp! For example: *"Do you know any jokes about Sodium hypobromite?"*

"NaBrO." Or "What's purple and 5000 miles long?" "The grape wall of China."

- Jokes can boost interest in <u>reading</u>: Children who are struggling with reading or reluctant to pick up a book are far more likely to pick up a joke book. Even if it isn't literature, jokes can be good practice for children who have difficulty in reading out loud. After all, jokes are meant to be shared!

What Are Our Categories?

There are four categories in this book, with 500 (and one) of the daddiest jokes in each – and one bonus joke hidden somewhere. The categories are:

1	Corniest Jokes	The most cornically classic Dad jokes to make everyone groan!
2	Terribly Bad (But Good) Jokes	Jokes that are so bad they become enjoyable again!
3	Knock Knock Jokes	A dad classic to make you sound aDOORable!
4	Punniest Puns	Wordplay to PUNish your Dad for all of his groan-worthy jokes!

How to Use This Book

The most important rule is to have fun with it. The rest is up to you! Here are the main points if you're a bit puzzled about where to get started.

- Each chapter has 125 jokes of the kind mentioned above.
- You can read the chapters in any order!
- Read them with your friends and family or simply read alone to learn as many jokes as possible.
- You can use the audio version in the car or over dinner, and you can have your book on you wherever you go! Look for opportunities to use it with everyone.

Some dos and don'ts.

Do

- ✓ Revisit old classic jokes after a while – find out your favorites!
- ✓ Get other people involved. Learning is fun in groups!
- ✓ Try and make up your own jokes!

Don't

- ✗ Ruin it for everyone – if you've already read the answer or heard the joke before, let someone else have a go!
- ✗ Show off. Remember, it's supposed to be fun!

Chapter One: Corniest Jokes

Here are 125 of the most cornically classic dad jokes to make everyone groan!
How many did you already know?

1. What do sprinters eat before a race?

   They don't eat anything because they fast!

2. What was that gig that cost just 45 cents?

   50 Cent and Nickelback.

3. Why did the student eat his homework?

   Because the teacher told him it was a piece of cake!

4. How do you fix a cracked pumpkin?

   With a pumpkin patch.

5. Why did Mozart sell his chickens?

   Because they kept saying, "Bach, Bach, Bach!"

6. "Dad, did you get a haircut?"

   "No, I got them all cut!"

7. How do you get a squirrel to like you?

   You act like a nut.

8. Why don't eggs tell jokes?

   Because they'll crack each other up.

9. "Dad, can you put my shoes on?"

   "No, I don't think they'll fit me."

10. "Dad, can you put the cat out?"

"I didn't know she was on fire."

11. Why did the picture go to jail?

Because it was framed.

12. Why was Cinderella thrown off the basketball team?

She ran away from the ball.

13. What do sea monsters eat for lunch?

Fish and ships.

14. Why was the horse so happy?

Because he lived in a stable environment.

15. What did the termite asked at the bar?

Where is the bar tender?

16. What time did the man go to the dentist?

At tooth hurt-y.

17. **How do you make a tissue dance?**

You put a little boogie in it.

18. **What do you call cheese that isn't yours?**

Nacho cheese.

19. **Why did the scarecrow win an award?**

It was outstanding in his field!

20. **What did mom say when she jumped out of the pantry?**

Supplies!

21. **Why did the cookie go to the nurse?**

It felt crummy.

22. **Which school subject was the witch's favorite?**

Spelling!

23. **What has ears but can't hear?**

A cornfield!

24. **Why did the teddy bear say no to dessert?**

Because she was stuffed!

25. **Why do bicycles fall over?**

Because they are two-tired!

26. **Why does Waldo wear stripes?**

Because he doesn't want to be spotted!

27. **What do you call a short criminal who escaped prison?**

A small medium at large!

28. Why did Mickey Mouse take a trip into space?

He wanted to find Pluto!

29. Why did the kid cross the playground?

To get to the other slide.

30. Why don't big cats play poker?

Because there are too many cheetahs.

31. Why couldn't the pirate play cards?

Because he was sitting on the deck!

32. What do you call two handbags running after each other?

A purse-uit!

33. What did baby corn say to the mama corn?

Where is popcorn?

34. Did you hear that rumor about butter?

Yes, and I'm going to spread it!!

35. What do you call a potato with glasses?

A spec-tater!

36. Why don't ghosts ever go trick or treating?

They have no body to go with!

37. What do you call a factory that manufactures really pleasing products?

A satisfactory!

38. Want to hear a joke about construction?

I'm still working on it!

39. **What do ghosts serve for dessert?**

I Scream.

40. **What do you call Han Solo making a Venn diagram?**

Comparison Ford.

41. **What do you call an elephant that doesn't matter?**

An irrelephant.

42. **What do you get from a pampered cow?**

Spoiled milk.

43. **What do taxidermists do for a living?**

Oh, you know... stuff.

44. **How do you think animals feel about having their organs sold in a butcher shop?**

Offal.

45. **I'm so good at sleeping that I can do it with my eyes closed!**

46. My wife told me I had to stop acting like a flamingo. So I had to put my foot down!

47. I told my wife she drew her eyebrows too high. She seemed surprised!

48. SON: I'll call you later.

   DAD: Don't call me later, call me Dad!

49. What do you do when balloons are hurt?

   You helium.

50. Why is Peter Pan always flying?

   He neverlands!

51. What's a thief's favorite type of shoes?

   Sneakers!

52. A woman was on trial for destruction of property, including expensive electric guitars.

   JUDGE: First offender?

   DEFENDANT: No, first a Gibson! Then a Fender!

53. What do you call a fake macaroni?

   An Impasta!

54. If two vegans get in a fight, is it still considered a beef?

55. What is a thesaurus' favorite dessert?

   Synonym buns.

56. How did the skeleton know it was going to rain?

   He felt it in his bones.

57. How does a Japanese dog say hi?

Konichihuahua.

58. How do you find Will Smith in the snow?

You look for fresh prints.

59. Why do ants never get ill?

They got these tiny anty-bodies.

60. I was going to share a vegetable joke, but it's corny.

61. What's red and smells like blue paint?

Red paint.

62. How many ears does Spock have?

Three. A left ear, a right ear, and the final front ear.

63. What did one ocean say to the other ocean?

Nothing, they just waved.

64. How many tickles does it take to make an octopus laugh?

Ten tickles.

65. Why kind of pasta do Spanish speakers prefer?

Aye Macaroni!

66. Why couldn't the mail person deliver any envelopes?

They were stationary.

67. What do you get if you cross an agnostic, an insomniac, and a dyslexic?

Someone who lays awake at night wondering if there's a Dog.

68. What does a zombie vegetarian eat?

GRRRAAAAIIIINNNNS!

69. PSYCHIC: That shirt is too small

EMPLOYEE: You didn't even try it on

PSYCHIC: I'm a medium

70. Which Avenger is the best at laundry?

Iron Man!

71. **Did you hear about the kidnapping at school?**

    It's okay though, he woke up!

72. **Why can't your nose be 12 inches long?**

    Because then it'll be a foot.

73. **DAUGHTER: Dad, can you make me a sandwich!**

    DAD: Poof, you're a sandwich!

74. **What do French people call a terrible Thursday?**

    A trajeudi

75. **What's the difference between a dirty bus stop and a lobster with breast implants?**

    One's a crusty bus station, and one's a busty crustacean

76. **What did the pirate say when he turned 80?**

    Aye matey!

77. What do you call a pompous villain coming down the stairs?

A condescending con descending.

78. Where do mailmen go on vacation?

Parcelona!

79. What do you do to dead chemists?

Your barium.

80. If I refuse to take a nap, would that mean I'm resisting arrest?

81. Why do cows have hooves instead of feet?

Because they lactose.

82. What's the tallest building in the city?

The library because it has the most stories.

83. Today, my son asked, "Can I have a bookmark?" and I burst into tears. 11 years old, and he still doesn't know my name is Brian, not Mark!

84. How do you make holy water?

You boil the hell out of it.

85. MOM: How do I look?

DAD: With your eyes.

86. What did the scarf say to the hat?

I'll hang around, you go on ahead.

87. What did the right eye say to the left eye?

Between you and me, something smells.

88. Can one bird make a pun?

No, but toucan.

89. How do you make Lady Gaga mad?

You poke her face.

90. Why can't you give Elsa a helium balloon?

Because she will let it go.

91. How do you catch a whole school of fish?

With bookworms.

92. What does a spy do when he gets cold?

He goes undercover.

93. I couldn't get a reservation at the library because they were fully booked.

94. Did you hear the story about the cheese that saved the world?

It was legend dairy.

95. Did you watch the new comic book movie?

It was very graphic!

96. What did the traffic light say to the crosswalk?

Don't look now, I'm changing!

97. What do you call a cow during an earthquake?

A milkshake.

98. I can't tell if I like this blender. It keeps giving me mixed results.

99. I can't believe that the penguin was denied bail. He's not even a flight risk!

100. Did you hear about the circus fire?

It was in tents.

101. Why do the French never order 2 eggs?

Because one egg is an oeuf.

102. How do lawyers say goodbye?

We'll be suing ya!

103. What did the paper say to the pencil?

You've got a good point!

104. What is the best Christmas present ever?

A broken drum – you can't beat it!

105. Do you want to hear a joke about paper?

Better not, I bet it's tearable.

106. **What's the best way to watch a fishing tournament?**

Live stream.

107. **I know a joke about pizza, but it's a little cheesy.**

108. **I don't trust anchovies. It's a little fishy.**

109. **When does a joke become a dad joke?**

When it becomes apparent.

110. **What sound does a witch's car make?**

Broom Broom.

111. **I wouldn't buy anything with Velcro.**

It's a total rip-off.

112. **What happens when a frog's car dies?**

He needs a jump, and if that doesn't work, he has to get it toad.

113. **Why do seagulls fly over the sea?**

Because if they flew over the bay, they'd be bagels.

114. **What do you call a cow with no legs?**

Ground beef.

115. **What do you call a cow that eats grass?**

A lawn-mooer.

116. **How do trees access the internet?**

They log in.

117. **What's the favorite computer place for astronauts to hang out?**

At the space bar.

118. **I don't play soccer because I enjoy the sport. I'm just doing it for kicks!**

119. **Why do bees have sticky hair?**

Because they use a honeycomb.

120. **Which state has the most streets?**

Rhode Island.

121. **What did the coffee report to the police?**

A mugging.

122. **What did the grape do when he got stepped on?**

He let out a little wine.

123. **What do you call a cow with a twitch?**

Beef Jerky.

124. **What musical instrument is found in the bathroom?**

A tuba toothpaste.

125. **Did you know that approximately 3.14% of sailors are pi-rates?**

Chapter Two: Terribly Bad (But Good) Jokes

125 jokes that are so bad they become enjoyable again!!

1. **SON: What rhymes with orange?**

   DAD: No, it doesn't!

2. **How did Darth Vader know what Luke got him for Christmas?**

   He felt his presents.

3. **I don't trust stairs. They're always up to something.**

4. **Why did the pirate walk the plank?**

   His dog was back on land.

5. **I was wondering why this Frisbee kept looking bigger and bigger. Then it**

   hit me.

6. 3 men are stranded in a boat with 4 cigarettes and no way to light them. So, they toss the 4th cigarette overboard, which makes the whole boat a cigarette lighter.

7. Well... That's a deep subject.

8. Can a kangaroo jump higher than a house?

   Of course. Houses can't jump.

9. I started a new business making yachts in my attic this year. The sails are going through the roof!

10. What's brown and sticky?

    A stick.

11. When is a door not a door?

    When it's ajar.

12. What did Obi-Wan say to Luke at a Chinese restaurant?

    "Use the fork, Luke."

13. What did the buffalo say to his son when he dropped him off at school?

    "Bison."

14. I used to be addicted to the hokey pokey. Then I turned myself around.

15. What did the horse say after it tripped?

    "Help! I've fallen, and I can't giddy up!"

16. What did Cinderella say when her photos did not show up?

    "Someday my prints will come!"

17. I've always hated elevators, so I've been taking steps to avoid them.

18. What does a nosey pepper do?

   It gets jalapeno business!

19. Why couldn't the pony sing himself a lullaby?

   He was a little hoarse.

20. Why do you never see elephants hiding in trees?

   Because they are really good at it.

21. Why is the grass so dangerous?

   It's full of blades.

22. What has four wheels and flies?

   A garbage truck!

23. Why can't you hear a pterodactyl going to the bathroom?

   Because the "P" is silent.

24. What do you get when you cross a centipede with a parrot?

   A walkie talkie.

25. I went to the zoo and saw a baguette in a cage.

The zookeeper said it was bread in captivity!

26. I like telling Dad jokes. Sometimes he laughs!

27. What do Kermit the Frog and Attila the Hun have in common?

They both have the same middle name.

28. At any given time, the urge to sing "the lion sleeps tonight" is just a whim away, a whim away, a whim away, a whim away!

29. How do astronomers organize a party?

They planet.

30. Arteries will always hold a special place in my heart.

31. Five out of four people admit they're bad with fractions!

32. I know several jokes about retired people, but none of them work!

33. If an English teacher is convicted of a crime and doesn't complete the sentence, is that a fragment?

34. DAD: I have found fault with an English word, and I need an entomologist!

MOM: Don't you mean an etymologist?

DAD: No, it's a bug, not a feature.

35. How did the police finally stop the paint thief?

They caught him red-handed.

36. Why did the hipster burn his tongue?

He drank his coffee before it was cool!

37. My ex-wife still misses me, but I'm scared because her aim is getting better!

38. Why are ghosts such bad liars?

You can see right through them.

39. How can you tell it's a dogwood tree?

From the bark.

40. How much does a pirate pay for corn?

A buccaneer.

41. Where does the king keep his armies?

In his sleevies.

42. How to be cool:

A) The cool sunglasses emoji.

B)

43. Why do scuba divers fall out of the boat backward?

Because if they fell forward, they'd still be in the boat!

44. What is the best way to communicate with a fish?

   Drop it a line.

45. I have the heart of a lion and a lifetime ban from the zoo!

46. Why is a baseball game a good place to go on a hot day?

   Because there are lots of fans.

47. My shepherd friend needed help to round up his 37 sheep. I said 40.

48. Why was 6 scared of 7?

   Because 7, 8, 9!

49. But why did 7 eat 9?

   Because you're supposed to eat 3 squared meals a day.

50. If ducks threw bread back at you, you'd have to duck.

51. Did you know that milk is the fastest liquid on Earth? It's pasteurized
   before you even see it.

52. Where do sharks go on vacation?

   Finland.

53. What would the couple name of Jack and Rose from the "*Titanic*" be?

    It doesn't matter, 'cause their ship sank.

54. Why does the clock break when it gets hungry?

    It goes back four seconds.

55. What's the definition of a will? Come on, guys, it's a dead giveaway!

56. REGULAR FRIEND: Tony, can you spell your name backward?

    DAD FRIEND: Sure... y not?

57. Have you heard about the sensitive burglar? He takes things personally.

58. You know what's really odd? Numbers not divisible by 2.

59. Who was the roundest knight at the Round Table?

    Sir Cumference. He ate 3.14 kilos of pi.

60. Where do frogs deposit their money?

    In a riverbank.

61. How can a leopard change his spots?

    By moving.

62. What do you call a bunch of chess players bragging about their games in a hotel lobby?

    Chess nuts boasting in an open foyer.

63. What's the difference between a guitar and a fish?

    You can't tuna fish.

64. Why do skunks celebrate Valentine's Day?

    They're very scent-imental.

65. A guy is taking his girlfriend to prom. He waits in the ticket line for a really long time but gets them. He goes to rent a limo. The rental line is really long, but he eventually does it. He goes to buy her flowers. The line at the florist is really long, but finally, he gets the flowers. At prom, she asks him to go get some punch. He goes to the refreshment table, and there's no punchline.

66. Why can't the bank keep a secret?

    It has too many tellers.

67. Why do spiders know so much?

    They can find everything on the web.

68. Making a new password:

    ME: beefstew

    COMPUTER: Sorry, password not stroganoff

69. My wife was furious at the fact that I have no sense of direction. So I packed up my stuff and right.

70. I ordered a chicken and an egg from Amazon. I'll let you know.

71. A slice of pie is $2.50 in Jamaica and $3.00 in the Bahamas. These are the pie rates of the Caribbean.

72. Why is a doctor always calm?

    Because they have a lot of patients.

73. **Where do bunnies go to eat pancakes?**

   To IHOP.

74. **What do you call an illegally parked frog?**

   Toad.

75. **What do you call the boss at Old McDonald's Farm?**

   The CIEIO.

76. **3 unwritten rules of life...**

   1.

   2.

   3.

77. **THIEF: I can't run anymore!**

   POLICEMAN: Sounds like you need arrest!

78. What's the difference between a poorly dressed man on a tricycle and a well-dressed man on a bicycle?

Attire!

79. What did one horse say to the other at the dance?

You mustang-o with me.

80. Why did the cookie cry?

Because his father was a wafer so long!

81. What's the king of all school supplies?

The ruler.

82. How do moths swim?

Using the butterfly stroke.

83. Where do baby cats learn to swim?

The kitty pool.

84. Why did Adele cross the road?

To say hello from the other side!

85. Which is faster, hot or cold?

Hot, because you can catch a cold.

86. Why did the belt get arrested?

He held up a pair of pants.

87. What kind of egg did the evil chicken lay?

A deviled egg.

88. Why don't oysters share their pearls?

Because they're shellfish.

89. What state do crayons go on vacation?

    Color-ado.

90. Why does Snoop Dogg always carry an umbrella?

    Fo' Drizzle.

91. I can cut down a tree only using my vision. I saw it with my own eyes.

92. Why are cats bad storytellers?

    Because they only have one tale.

93. Bacon and eggs walk into a bar. The bartender says, "Sorry, we don't

    serve breakfast."

94. What do you call a baby monkey?

    A chimp off the old block.

95. Why should you wear two pairs of pants when you golf?

    In case you get a hole-in-one.

96. Did you hear about the two guys who stole a calendar? They each got six months.

97. Why can't a leopard hide?

Because he's always spotted.

98. What did the shoe say to the confused hat?

You go on ahead.

99. What did the drummer name his twin daughters?

Anna 1, Anna 2!

100. Why did the invisible man turn down the job offer?

He couldn't see himself doing it.

101. What do you get when you cross fish and an elephant?

Swimming trunks.

102. Which day do chickens hate the most?

Friday.

103. Why do geologists hate their jobs?

They get taken for granite.

104. How well did I hang up that picture?

I nailed it.

105. Why is it hard to explain puns to kleptomaniacs?

They always take things literally.

106. Why are skeletons so calm?

Because nothing gets under their skin.

107. The recipe said, "Set the oven to 180 degrees." But now I can't open it because the door faces the wall.

108. What did the fisherman say to the magician?

    Pick a cod, any cod.

109. Did you hear about the restaurant on the moon? Great food, no atmosphere.

110. How many apples grow on trees?

    All of them!

111. How do celebrities stay cool?

    They have many fans.

112. What do you call it when Batman skips church?

    Christian Bale.

113. What do you get when you cross a snowman and a vampire?

    Frostbite.

114. Server: Sorry about your wait.

    Dad: Are you saying I'm fat?

115. Do I enjoy making courthouse puns?

    Guilty.

116. HOSTESS: Do you have reservations?

    DAD: No. I'm confident I want to eat here.

117. I dreamed about drowning in an ocean made out of orange soda last night. It took me a while to work out that it was just a Fanta sea.

118. What do you call a hippie's wife?

Mississippi.

119. I was diagnosed as colorblind the other day, and it really came out of the purple!

120. DAD: I want a book by Shakespeare?

BOOKSELLER: Of course, sir, which one?

DAD: William.

121. Why did the coach go to the bank?

To get his quarterback.

122. What do you call a row of people lifting mozzarella?

A cheesy pick-up line.

123. I'll never date another apostrophe. The last one was too possessive.

124. I dig, you dig, we dig, she digs, he digs, they dig. It's not a beautiful poem, but it's very deep.

125. Did you hear about the guy who invented the knock-knock joke? He won the 'no-bell' prize.

Chapter Three: Knock Knock Jokes

A dad classic to make you sound aDOORable!

1. "Knock knock!" "Who's there?" "Hatch." "Hatch who?" "Bless you."

2. "Knock knock!" "Who's there?" "Tank." "Tank who?" "You're welcome."

3. "Knock knock!" "Who's there?" "Nana." "Nana who?" "Nana your business."

4. "Knock knock!" "Who's there?" "Adore." "Adore who?" "Adore is between us. Open up!"

5. "Knock knock!" "Who's there?" "Cargo." "Cargo who?" "You're wrong! Car go 'beep beep'!"

6. "Knock knock!" "Who's there?" "Alpaca." "Alpaca who?" "Alpaca the trunk, you pack the suitcase!"

7. "Knock knock!" "Who's there?" "A little old lady." "A little old lady who?" "Oh, wow, I never knew you could yodel!"

8. "Knock knock!" "Who's there?" "Keith!" "Keith who?"" "Keith me, my thweet preenth!"

9. "Knock knock!" "Who's there?" "Boo." "Boo who?" Hey, don't cry!

10. "Knock knock!" "Who's there?" "Cantaloupe! "Cantaloupe who?" "Cantaloupe with you to Vegas, I don't see you that way!".

11. "Knock knock!" "Who's there?" Spell. Spell who?" "W-H-O."

12. "Knock knock!" "Who's there?" "Cash." "Cash who?" "No thanks, I'm allergic to nuts!"

13. "Knock knock!" "Who's there?" "Olive."" Olive who?" "Olive you too!"

14. "Knock knock!" "Who's there?" "Ho-ho." "Ho-ho who?" "Wow, that's a bad Santa impression!"

15. "Knock knock!" "Who's there?" "Owls say." "Owls say who?" "So, they do!"

16. "Knock knock!" "Who's there?" "Déja." "Déja who?" "Knock knock!"

17. "Knock knock!" "Who's there?" "Leena." "Leena who?" "Leena little closer and I will tell you!"

18. "Knock knock!" "Who's there?" "Witches." "Witches who?" "Witches the way to the store."

19. "Knock knock!" "Who's there?" "Beets!" "Beets who?" "Beets me!"

20. "Knock knock!" "Who's there?" "To." "To who?" "Actually, it's 'to whom.'"

21. "Knock knock!" "Who's there?" "Broken pencil." "Broken pencil who?" "Never mind, there's no point!"

22. "Knock knock!" "Who's there?" "Zany." "Zany who?" "Zany body home?"

23. "Knock knock!" "Who's there?" "Iran." "Iran who?" "Iran over someone! Help!"

24. "Knock knock!" "Who's there?" "FBI." "FB…" "We ask the questions here."

25. "Knock knock!" "Who's there?" "Mikey." "Mikey who?" "Mikey got lost; open the door!"

26. "Knock knock!" "Who's there?" "Cook." "Cook who?" You sound crazy, yes!"

27. "Knock knock!" "Who's there?" "Orange." "Orange who?" "Orange you even going to open the door!"

28. "Knock knock!" "Who's there?" "Armageddon." "Armageddon who?" "Armageddon a little bored." "Let's go out."

29. "Knock knock!" "Who's there?" "Stopwatch." "Stopwatch who?" "Stopwatcha doin' and open the stupid door."

30. "Knock knock!" "Who's there?" "Rough." " Rough who?" "Rough, rough, rough! It's your dog!"

31. "Knock knock!" "Who's there?" "Jester." "Jester who?" "Jester silly old man!"

32. "Knock knock!" "Who's there?" "Egg." "Egg who?" "Eggcited to see me?"

33. "Knock knock!" "Who's there?" "Twit." "Twit who?" "Did anyone else hear an owl?"

34. "Knock knock!" "Who's there?" "Kermit." "Kermit who?" "Kermit a crime, and you'll get locked up!"

35. "Knock knock!" "Who's there?" "Ice cream!" "Ice cream who?" "Ice cream if you don't let me in!"

36. "Knock knock!" "Who's there?" "Frank!" "Frank who?" "Frank you for being my friend!"

37. "Knock knock!" "Who's there?" "Sorry." "Sorry who?" "Sorry, wrong door!"

38. "Knock knock!" "Who's there?" "Abby." "Abby who?" "Abby birthday to you!"

39. "Knock knock!" "Who's there?" "Burglar." " Burglar who?" "Burglars don't knock!"

40. "Knock knock!" "Who's there?" "Fiddle." "Fiddle who?" "Fiddle make you happy; I'll tell you!"

41. "Knock knock!" "Who's there?" "Isabelle." "Isabelle who?" "Isabelle working?"

42. "Knock knock!" "Who's there?" "House." "House who?" "House you doing?"

43. "Knock knock!" "Who's there?" "Europe." " Europe who?" "Europe early this morning!"

44. "Knock knock!" "Who's there?" "Grub." " Grub who?" "Grub hold of my hand, and let's go!"

45. "Knock knock!" "Who's there?" "Bruce." "Bruce who?" "Bruce easily, don't hit me!"

46. "Knock knock!" "Who's there?" "Jamaica." "Jamaica who? "Jamaica mistake?" "Just let me in!"

47. "Knock knock!" "Who's there?" "Justin." "Justin who?" "Justin the neighborhood, thought I'd drop by."

48. "Knock knock!" "Who's there?" "Britney Spears." "Britney Spears who?" "Knock, knock—oops, I did it again."

49. "Knock knock!" "Who's there?" "Will." "Will who?" "Will you let me in?"

50. "Knock knock!" "Who's there?" "Thermos." "Thermos who?" "Thermos be a better way to get through to you."

51. "Knock knock!" "Who's there?" "Hey." "" "Hey who?" "Hey ho, hey ho, it's off to work we go!"

52. "Knock knock!" "Who's there?" "Woo." "Woo who?" "Don't get so excited, it's just a joke."

53. "Knock knock!" "Who's there?" "Cows go." "Cow's go who?" "No! Cows go moo!"

54. "Knock knock!" "Who's there?" "Dishes!" "Dishes who?" "Dishes the police. Come out with your hands up."

55. "Knock knock!" "Who's there?" "Ears." "Ears who?" "Ears another knock knock joke for you!"

56. "Knock knock!" "Who's there?" "Interrupting cow!" "Inter--" "Moo!"

57. "Knock knock!" "Who's there?" "Needle." " Needle who?" "Needle little help getting in the door!"

58. "Knock knock!" "Who's there?" "Hike." "Hike who?" "I didn't know you liked Japanese poetry!"

59. "Knock knock!" "Who's there?" "I am." " I am who?" "You tell me!"

60. "Knock knock!" "Who's there?" "Oink, oink." " Oink oink who?" "Make up your mind—are you a pig or an owl?!"

61. "Knock knock!" "Who's there?" "Figs." " Figs who?" "Figs the doorbell, it's broken!"

62. "Knock knock!" "Who's there?" "Radio." " Radio who?" "Radio not, here I come!"

63. "Knock knock!" "Who's there?" "Art." " Art who?" "R2-D2."

64. "Knock knock!" "Who's there?" "No one." No one who?" "*Remains silent*

65. "Knock knock!" "Who's there?" "Annie. Annie who?" "Annie one you like!"

66. "Knock knock!" "Who's there?" "Merry. Merry who?" "Merry Christmas!"

67. "Knock knock!" "Who's there?" "Iva. Iva who?" "Iva sore hand from knocking! "

68. "Knock knock!" "Who's there?" "Dozen. Dozen who?" "Dozen anybody want to let me in?"

69. "Knock knock!" "Who's there?" "Needle. Needle who?" "Needle little money for the movies."

70. "Knock knock!" "Who's there?" "Henrietta. Henrietta who?" "Henrietta worm that was in his apple."

71. "Knock knock!" "Who's there?" "Avenue. Avenue who?" "Avenue knocked on this door before?"

72. "Knock knock!" "Who's there?" "Harry. Harry who?" "Harry up, it's cold out here!"

73. "Knock knock!" "Who's there?" "A herd. A herd who?" "A herd you were home, so I came over!"

74. "Knock knock!" "Who's there?" "Otto. Otto who?" "Otto know. I've got amnesia."

75. "Knock knock!" "Who's there?" "King Tut. King Tut who?" "King Tut-key fried chicken!"

76. "Knock knock!" "Who's there?" "Lettuce. Lettuce who?" "Lettuce in it's cold out here."

77. "Knock knock!" "Who's there?" "Noah. Noah who?" "Noah good place we can get something to eat?"

78. "Knock knock!" "Who's there?" "Robin. Robin who?" "Robin the piggy bank again."

79. "Knock knock!" "Who's there?" "Dwayne. Dwayne who?" "Dwayne the bathtub, It's overflowing!"

80. "Knock knock!" "Who's there?" "Leon." "Leon who?" "Leon me when you're not strong!"

81. "Knock knock!" "Who's there?" "Annie." "Annie who?" "Annie thing you can do, I can better!"

82. "Knock knock!" "Who's there?" "Quiche." "Quiche who?" "Can I have a hug and a quiche?"

83. "Knock knock!" "Who's there?" "A leaf." "A leaf who?" "A leaf you alone if you leaf me alone."

84. "Knock knock!" "Who's there?" "Ice cream soda." "Ice cream soda who?" "Ice scream soda people can hear me!"

85. "Knock knock!" "Who's there?" "Candice." "Candice who?" "Candice joke get any worse?"

86. "Knock knock!" "Who's there?" "Anita." "Anita who?" "Anita drink of water, so please let me in!"

87. "Knock knock!" "Who's there?" "Banana." "Banana who?" "Knock knock!" "Who's there?" "Banana." "Banana who?" "Knock knock!" "Who's there?" "Orange." "Orange who?" "Orange you glad I didn't say banana again?"

88. "Knock knock!" "Who's there?" "Alex." "Alex who?" "Alex-plain when you open the door!"

89. "Knock knock!" "Who's there?" "Hawaii." "Hawaii who?" "I'm fine, Hawaii you?"

90. "Knock knock!" "Who's there?" "June." "June who?" "June know how long I've been knocking out here?"

91. "Knock knock!" "Who's there?" "Oscar." "Oscar who?" "Oscar silly question and get a silly answer!"

92. "Knock knock!" "Who's there?" "Conrad." "Conrad who?" "Conrad-ulations!" That was a good knock-knock joke!"

93. "Knock knock!" "Who's there?" "Mustache." "Mustache who?" "Mustache you a question, but I'll shave it for later!"

94. "Knock knock!" "Who's there?" "Ya." "Ya who?" "No thanks, I use Google."

95. "Knock knock!" "Who's there?" "Control Freak." "Contro- Okay, now you say control freak who?"

96. "Knock knock!" "Who's there?" "Theodore." "Theodore who?" "Theodore wasn't opened, so I knocked."

97. "Knock knock!" "Who's there?" "Alec." "Alec who?" "Alec it when you ask me questions." "

98. "Knock knock!" "Who's there?" "Cereal." "Cereal who?" "Cereal pleasure to meet you!"

99. "Knock knock!" "Who's there?" "Europe." "Europe who?" "No, you're a poo!"

100. "Knock knock!" "Who's there?" "Double." "Double who?" "W!"

101. "Knock knock!" "Who's there?" "Kenya." "Kenya who?" "Kenya feel the love tonight?"

102. "Knock knock!" "Who's there?" "Interrupting sloth." "Interrupting sloth who?" *20 seconds of silence* "Slooooooooooth!"

103. "Knock knock!" "Who's there?" "Ida." "Ida who?" "Uhm, I'm sure it's pronounced Idaho."

104. "Knock knock!" "Who's there?" "Cabbage." "Cabbage who?" "You expect a cabbage to have a last name?"

105. "Knock knock!" "Who's there?" "You didn't remember me!"

106. "Knock knock!" "Who's there?" "Razor." "Razor who?" "Razor hands and dance the boogie!"

107. "Knock knock!" "Who's there?" "Sweden." "Sweden who?" "Sweden sour chicken!"

108. "Knock knock!" "Who's there?" "Opportunity." "Opportunity doesn't knock twice!"

109. "Knock knock!" "Who's there?" "I smell mop." "I smell mop who?" "Ew."

110. "Knock knock!" "Who's there?" "Honeybee." "Honeybee who?" "Honeybee a dear and open up, will you?"

111. "Knock knock!" "Who's there?" "Says." "Says who?" "Says me, that's who!"

112. "Knock knock!" "Who's there?" "Alice." "Alice who?" "Alice so quiet." "Let's make some noise!"

113. "Knock knock!" "Who's there?" "Doctor." "Doctor who?" "No, no, just the regular doctor."

114. "Knock knock!" "Who's there?" "Amish." "Amish who?" "Really, you're a shoe?" "Uh, okay."

115. "Knock knock!" "Who's there?" "Luke." "Luke who?" "Luke through the keyhole and see!"

116. "Knock knock!" "Who's there?" "Amos." "Amos who?" "A mosquito!"

117. "Knock knock!" "Who's there?" "Odysseus." "Odysseus who?" "Odysseus the last straw!"

118. "Knock knock!" "Who's there?" "A Mayan." "A Mayan who?" "A Mayan in the way?"

119. "Knock knock!" "Who's there?" "Icing." "Icing who?" "Icing so loudly so everyone can hear me!"

120. "Knock knock!" "Who's there?" "Tennis." "Tennis who?" "Tennis five plus five!"

121. "Knock knock!" "Who's there?" "..." "...uncomfortable silence who?"

122. "Knock knock!" "Who's there?" "Gorilla." "Gorilla who?" "Gorilla me a hamburger!"

123. "Knock knock!" "Who's there?" "Snow." "Snow who?" "Snow use, I forgot my name again."

124. "Knock knock!" "Who's there?" "Nicholas." "Nicholas who?" "A Nicholas is not much money these days."

125. "Knock knock!" "Who's there?" "Haven." "Haven who?" "Haven you heard enough of these knock-knock jokes?"

Chapter Four: Punniest Puns

Wordplay to PUNish your Dad for all of his groan-worthy jokes!

1. I tell dad jokes, but I have no kids...I'm a faux pa!

2. Two lobsters are chilling in a tank. One says to the other, "Do you know how to drive this thing?"

3. The difference between a numerator and a denominator is a short line. Only a fraction of people will understand this!

4. The math book looked sad because it was full of problems!

5. I don't really call for funerals that start before noon. I guess I'm just not a mourning person!

6. 100 years ago, everyone owned a horse, and only the rich had cars. Today everyone has cars and only the rich own horses. How the stables have turned!

7. I didn't like my beard at first, but then it grew on me.

8. "Orion's belt is a big waist of space." "Terrible joke, only three stars."

9. A French guy was showing his friend his boats.

   "This is Un, this is Deux, this is Trois, This is Quatre. This is Six."

   So his friend asks, "Hey, where is the fifth?

   "It cinq."

10. My friend really changed once she became a vegetarian. It's like I've never

    seen herbivore.

11. A priest, an Imam, and a Rabbit walk into a blood bank. The Rabbit says,

    "I might be a Typo."

12. Time flies like an arrow. Fruit flies like a banana.

13. I, for one, like Roman numerals.

14. I could tell you a chemistry joke, but I know I wouldn't get a reaction.

15. I wish Medusa would stop objectifying people.

16. The tenth Fast and Furious movie should be called Fast 10: Your

    Seatbelts.

17. A man was hit on the head with a can of Coke, but it was okay because it

    was a soft drink.

18. You've heard of alphabet soup, now get ready for Times New Ramen!

19. People who get abducted by extraterrestrials can't really tell anyone.

    They must feel so alienated.

20. I just bought a thesaurus from the bookstore. However, when I got home,

    I found that all the pages were blank! I have no words to describe how

    angry I am.

21. If you put a picture of yourself in a locket, you could say you are...

    Independent!

22. The key to a good mailman joke is the delivery.

23. Once on a field trip, I visited a prison library. It had prose and cons.

24. A good artist knows where to draw the line.

25. The rotation of Earth really makes my day!

26. I got robbed on an elevator. That was wrong on so many levels!

27. Harry Potter can't tell the difference between his potions' pot and his

    best friend because they're both cauldron!

28. Opera enthusiasts are the Fandom of the Opera.

29. Shakespeare used to sell off-season camping gear. It was the winter of

    his discount tents!

30. No matter how kind you are, German children are kinder!

31. There's nothing funny about mitosis jokes. Once you say one, everyone

    splits.

32. I named my three kittens Fork, Spoon, and Knife, because they're catlery.

33. Seven days without a pun makes one weak.

34. I just looked outside to check the patriarchy, and apparently, it's reigning men.

35. A man entered his house and was absolutely delighted because someone had stolen all his lamps.

36. I had a job crushing cans, but I quit because it was soda-pressing.

37. Leather armor is the best for sneaking because it's made of hide.

38. Rest in peace, boiled water. You will be mist.

39. Serial killer jokes aren't funny unless you execute them well.

40. Writing with a broken pencil is pointless.

41. Weddings are so emotional even the cake is in tiers!

42. A man was hospitalized with 6 plastic horses inside him. The doctor described his condition as stable!

43. I'm reading a book about anti-gravity. It's impossible to put down!

44. My friend keeps saying, "cheer up, man, it could be worse, you could be stuck underground in a hole full of water." I know he means well.

45. Justice is a dish best served cold. If it were served warm, it would be justwater.

46. Don't trust atoms. They make up everything!

47. Looks like I lost an electron, I should keep a better ion them.

48. I knew a woman who owned a taser! She was stunning!

49. A student asked his teacher if his grades were excellent in Spanish. She said C.

50. I had to get glasses for my phone because I lost all the contacts.

51. I saw an ad for a $1 radio, volume stuck on high. How was I supposed to turn that down?

52. I changed my iPod name to Titanic. It's syncing now.

53. I did a theatrical performance about puns. It was a play on words.

54. I saw a beaver movie last night, it was the best dam movie I've ever seen.

55. To tell the difference between a chemist and a plumber, you ask them to pronounce "unionized."

56. Giant squid jokes are Kraken me up!

57. To whoever stole my copy of Microsoft Office, I will find you. You have my Word!

58. This graveyard is overcrowded. People are dying to get in.

59. It takes guts to be an organ donor.

60. Most people are shocked when they find out how bad an electrician I am.

61. I tried to catch some fog, but I mist.

62. I don't know why Marvel hasn't tried to put advertisements on Hulk. He is essentially a giant banner.

63. I gave all my dead batteries away today... Free of charge!

64. I named my printer Bob Marley because it's always jammin'.

65. A friend said she did not understand cloning. I told her that makes two of us.

66. I want to be cremated as it is my last hope for a smoking hot body.

67. Did you hear about the school that converted to Marxism? I heard they don't have any classes.

68. Novice pirates make terrible singers because they can't hit the high seas.

69. Jokes about communism are only funny if you share them with everyone.

70. I really wanted a camouflage shirt, but I couldn't find one.

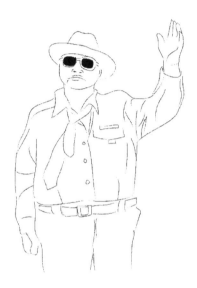

71. What did the dying composer say? I'll be Bach.

72. Where do you imprison a skeleton? In a rib cage.

73. The cross-eyed teacher just couldn't control her pupils.

74. The night club nearby recently contracted a carpenter. He's really tearing up the dance floor.

75. I'm glad I know sign language, it's pretty handy.

76. George's model airplane hobby really took off.

77. Simba was walking slow, so I told him Mufasa.

78. Arranging Goliath's funeral was a giant undertaking.

79. Rick Astley will let you borrow any of his Pixar collection DVDs, but he will never give you UP.

80. I was going to tell you a joke about infinity, but it didn't have an ending!

81. Met my wife on a dating site and I don't know, we just clicked.

82. Once upon a time, a lumberjack wandered into a magical forest to cut a tree. As he swung his ax, the tree said: "Don't cut me down, I'm a talking tree!" The lumberjack replied, "And you will dialogue."

83. A New Year's resolution is something that goes in one year and out the other.

84. My son didn't tell me he ate some glue. His lips were sealed.

85. Stairs are useful, and all, but elevators are really some next-level technology.

86. I couldn't find my favorite tv show. I guess it was Lost.

87. I know this pun about cows, but it's a little offensive, so I won't say it. I don't want there to be any beef between us.

88. The overreacting Watermelon was being melondramatic.

89. The invention of dynamite sure was groundbreaking.

90. I had a bad day, so I brought a crate of booze up to my apartment in the elevator because I needed something to lift my spirits.

91. I hate negative numbers and will stop at nothing to avoid them.

92. The cost of the space program is astronomical.

93. Puberty is like my shower. It takes a really long time to get hot.

94. Did you hear about the guy whose whole left side was cut off? He's all

right now.

95. I think Santa has a riverfront property in Brazil. All our presents came

from Amazon this year.

96. I tried asking my dentist out, but she brushed me off. Don't worry, it's

her floss.

97. My son swallowed some coins, and I took him to a hospital. When I asked

the nurse how he was, she said there was no change yet.

98. My dog has an attitude. He is a cocky spaniel.

99. Wizard dating tip: always look for girls at the beach. Sand witches are the

tastiest.

100. I sold my vacuum cleaner—it was just gathering dust!

101. Ed has no girlfriend as Sheeran away.

102. The royal family moved into my neighborhood. They live Tudors down.

103. I got arrested at the Farmers Market for disturbing the peas.

104. My wife told me moose were falling from the sky. I told her, "It's reindeer."

105. Telekinesis is not a handy skill.

106. A photon walks into a hotel with no luggage and goes to check-in. The bellhop asks if he has any bags. The photon replies, "No, sir; I'm traveling light."

107. The skeleton was trying tibia little humerus.

108. In my bedroom, the curtains were drawn, but the rest of the furniture was real.

109. I once got into so much debt that I couldn't even afford my electricity bills. They were the darkest times of my life.

110. Ladies, if he can't appreciate your fruit jokes, you need to let that mango.

111. I had a neck brace fitted years ago, and I've never looked back since.

112. You know, people say they pick their nose, but I feel like I was just born with mine.

113. Those who jump off into the Paris river are in Seine.

114. Going to bed with music gave me a sound sleep.

115. Broken puppets for sale. No strings attached.

116. Just burned 2,000 calories. That's the last time I leave brownies in the oven while I nap.

117. Go to Italy to Rome around and pasta time.

118. A man who took an airline company to court after losing his luggage has lost his case.

119. No one knew I had a dental implant until it came out in a conversation.

120. I told a pun in civics class. It went down in history.

121. Organ donors put their heart into it.

122. I live in an airport, but when the security guard comes at night, Heathrows me out.

123. Shout out to the people that don't know what the opposite of in is!

124. I broke my right thumb today, but on the other hand I'm completely fine.

125. I started a business breeding chicken, but I'm struggling to make hens meet.

Conclusion

Congratulations! You made it through 500 of the cheesiest dad jokes across 4 categories! I bet you feel like your brain is a little fried after that!

What's that? Did we promise 501? Okay, here's the last one and one of our personal favorites!

501.ME: I am terrified of the vertical axes

THERAPIST: Why?

ME: *Screams*

These categories and facts were hand-picked for dads, but their spouses, their kids, and teens can use them any time too! Everyone should train their funny bones! A world without laughter doesn't promise for a very bright future, and we hope we have helped with that!

What other jokes would you like to see in the future? Let us know in your reviews, or maybe make up your own! Our team has been really excited throughout making this book, and we hope we excited and inspired you too.

We look forward to seeing you join us in our next learning adventure.

The End

(Nearly)

Reviews are not easy to come by.

As an independent author with a tiny marketing budget, I rely on readers, like you, to leave a short review on Amazon.

Even if it's just a sentence or two!

Printed in Great Britain
by Amazon